How to Cook Everything with a CAST IRON SKILLET

A Beginner's Guide

- Part 1 -

JEREMY SCHAFFER

CONTENTS

Granny's Sausage and Gravy

Tomato Gravy

<u>SOUP, STEW, GUMBO & CHILI</u>

Southern Greens Soup

Tex-Mex Minestrone

New England Clam Chowder

Long Island Clam Chowder

Clam, Sausage, and Corn Chowder

McNew's Okra Stew

Southern Brunswick Stew

Beef in Guinness

Oven Beef Stew

Chicken Stew with Fluffy Dumplings

Polish Pork and Cabbage Stew (Bigos)

Catfish Courtbouillon

Cioppino (San Francisco Italian Fish Stew)

Chicken Filé Gumbo

Duck, Oyster, and Andouille Gumbo

Gumbo Z'Herbes

Veggie Chili in Cast Iron

Tennessee White Chili

Chef Boy-R-Bob's Chili Verde

Flat-Iron Cherry-Bomb Chili Texas-Style Red

"Cin-Chili" Chili

Lady Bug Chili

Jim Maturo's Chili

THE MAIN COURSE

Skillet Cauliflower-Feta Pizza

Crustless Quiche Chipotle

French Cassoulet, Vegetarian Style

Spicy Pan-Roasted Green Beans (Sem Masala)

Tofu–Bok Choy Stir-fry with Oyster Mushrooms

Thanksgiving Day Vegetarian Casserole

Fish Tacos with Mango Slaw and Avocado Crema

Cornmeal Fried Catfish over Black-eyed Pea Salad with Pickled Jalapeño Relish

Skillet-Fried Porgies

Seafood Boil

Nannie's Catfish Cakes

Come Back Sauce

Pan-Fried Rocky Mountain Trout with Toasted Hazelnuts

Pan-Roasted Sea Bass with Chive-Garlic Compound Butter

Iron Skillet Roasted Mussels

Shrimp with Fresh Basil, Thai Style

Black Pepper Skillet Shrimp (Meen Varuval)

Savannah Red Rice

Barbecue Shrimp over Rice

Scallop Pie

Casserole of Scallops, Chestnut Farro, and Hen of the Woods Mushrooms with Sorghum Veal Glacé

Mother's Favorite Fried Chicken

Spatchcock Chicken

Nona's Chicken

Grilled Chicken with Citrus Salsa

Smothered Chicken with Butter Beans

Stuffed Garlic Chicken Breasts

Chicken with Artichoke Hearts, Olives, and Capers

Tom's Widely Known Wayfarer Chicken Curry

Chicken Tagine

Tennessee Valley Jambalaya

Seared Teal Breasts

Sage and Citrus-Braised Duck

Duck Breast with Sugar Snap Peas and Mushrooms

Skillet Fried Rabbit with Gravy

Tender Venison Roast

Braised Breast of Grouse

Seared Pepper Steak with Bourbon-Shallot Sauce

Cast Iron Grilled Steaks with Blue Cheese Butter

Pan-fried Fajita Steaks

Sukiyaki

Bourbon Barrel Pepper Pot Roast

Rolled Flank Steak

Tomato Reduction Recipe

Part Pesto

Steak, Kidney, and Mushroom Pie

Grillades

All-American Short Ribs

Shepherd's Pie

Seared Pork Chops with Caramelized Apples and Onions

Pan Pork with Rapid Ratatouille

Lomo de Puerco Asado (Roasted Pork Loin)

Carnitas (Mexican Pulled Pork Tacos)

Braised Pork Shoulder with Star Anise

Indoor Pulled Pork with North Carolina Vinegar Sauce

North Carolina Coleslaw

COOKING OUTDOORS

Grilled Margherita Pizza

Seared Rosemary and Garlic Porterhouse with Browned Butter

Pepper Steak al Fresco

Grilled Veal Chops

Cast Iron Beer Can Chicken

Pan-Grilled Halibut with Tarragon Butter Sauce

Sandy Beach Shrimp Tacos with Mango Salsa

Rosemary-and-Garlic Grilled Shrimp

Deep-Fried Catfish

Herbed Grilled Eggplant

Grilled Okra

Mark's Summer Bean and Vegetable Surprise

Grilled Sweet Potatoes with Lime-Cilantro Dressing

Heat-Wave Bread

Sweet Potato Soufflé

Roast Cornish Game Hen with Wild Rice Stuffing

Bacon-Wrapped Stuffed Turkey Breast

Stuffed French Toast

Buttermilk Syrup

Campfire Chicken Cacciatore

Bacon-Herb Wrapped Pork Tenderloin

Ham, Turkey, and Cheese Bread

Feather Light Rolls

Dutch Oven Danish Cake

Hot Lava Chocolate Cake for Two

Cow Patty Raspberry Fudge Cake

Pam's Bean Hole Beans

Bean Hole Peach Cobbler

George's Bean Hole Roast AND Veggies

SIDES

Poke Salat

Wilted Lettuce Salad

Scott's Collards

Squash Puppies

Summer Squash Casserole

Zucchini Pancakes with Red Pepper-Yogurt Sauce

Fried Corn

Roasted Corn Pudding

Sauté of Corn, Brown Rice, and Fresh Basil

Julia's Succotash

South Coast Hominy

Southern Style String Beans

Rajma (North Indian Red Kidney Beans)

Oacie's Baked Beans

Southern Fried Okra

Sweet and Tangy Glazed Carrots with Cranberries

Caramelized Brussels Sprouts

Nurit's Noodle Pudding

Lyonnaise Potatoes

Cast Iron-Roasted Red Potatoes with Rosemary and Onion

NOTHIN' BUT CORNBREAD

This Ain't No Yankee Cornbread

Sour Cream Cornbread

Elizabeth's Scalded Cornbread

Mayonnaise Cornbread for Two

Aunt Jimmie's Yeast Cornbread

Mrs. Loyd's Mexican Cornbread

Vidalia Cornbread

Cranberry-Orange Cornbread with Orange "Butter"

Bacon and Green Onion Skillet Cornbread

Corn Fingers

Smoked Sausage Hot Water Corn Cakes

Doc Havron's Hush Puppies

Mrs. Reed's Cornbread Dressing

Amish Chicken Cornbread Bake

Buffalo Chicken Cornbread with Blue Cheese Salad

Chicken and Dressing Skillet Bake

White Chicken Chili with Cheddar Hush-Puppy Crust

Chicken Taco Cornbread Wedges with Ranchero Cilantro Drizzle

Buffalo Chicken Cornbread with Blue Cheese Mayonnaise

Monte Cristo Cornbread Skillet Supper

Bacon and Gorgonzola Cornbread Sliders with Chipotle Mayo

Upside-Down Salsa Cornbread

Reuben Casserole with Cornbread

Festive Good Luck Cornbread Skillet

The Crescent City Skillet

Ancho Shrimp on Smoked Gouda Corncakes

Cornbread Supreme with Shrimp

DESSERTS, BISCUITS & BREAD

Lemon-Lavender Pound cakes

Pineapple Upside-Down Cakes One by One

Blueberry-Ginger-Peach Upside-Down Cake with Ginger Whipped Cream

Cranberry Apple Pie

Blueberry-Peach Skillet Pie

Worth-the-Effort Tarte Tatin

Rustic Spiced Peach Tart with Almond Pastry

Simple Berry Skillet Cobbler

Cherry Clafouti

New Orleans Pralines

Peanut Butter Fudge

Dixie Peanut Brittle

Giant Cookie–in-a-Pan

Buttermilk Drop Biscuits

Blushing Drop Biscuits

<u>Quick Rolls</u>

<u>Spoon Rolls</u>

<u>Brother Anselm's Popovers</u>

<u>Crusty White Peasant-Style Pot Bread</u>

<u>Maggie Doherty's Irish Soda Bread</u>

BREAKFAST

What says breakfast better than a cast iron skillet filled with crispy bacon? Well, we think breakfast is far more than bacon, and this chapter offers a wonderful selection of egg dishes, pancakes, and breakfast breads to start your day off right!

Seasonal Breakfast Frittata

SEASONAL BREAKFAST FRITTATA

serves 8

This easy-to-prepare dish has been a longtime breakfast favorite in the Ryder-Topalian household. Since the ingredients can be changed according to the season, it's always a snap to make with whatever you have in your fridge or whatever is ripe in your garden. "This is my go-to recipe for whenever we have houseguests. It's beautiful when it comes out of the oven, with its puffed-up golden brown top, and it provides everyone with a satisfying start to their day," says Tracey Ryder, cofounder of Edible Communities, a network of more than 65 regional food magazines across the United States and Canada devoted to the local foods movement.

$3/4$ pound bulk mild Italian pork sausage or chorizo

6   large eggs

1   cup heavy cream

Salt, freshly ground black pepper, and red pepper flakes

2   large handfuls baby spinach, Swiss chard, or arugula, washed and spun dry

8   ounces feta cheese, crumbled

1   large ripe tomato, coarsely chopped (optional)

1. Preheat the oven to 375°.

2. Cook the sausage in a 10-inch cast iron skillet over medium heat, stirring often, until it crumbles and is no longer pink. Remove the sausage and drain on paper towels. Drain all the fat from the skillet, but do not wipe the skillet clean because you want some of the sausage flavor left behind.

3. Place the eggs, cream, and salt and black and red pepper to taste in a large bowl; whisk until the mixture is foamy. Add the sausage, spinach, feta, and, if desired, tomato and stir until all the ingredients are fully incorporated and coated with the egg mixture.

4. Pour the egg mixture into the skillet and cook over medium heat until it begins to set and hold together around the outside edge. Place the skillet in the oven and bake until the top of the frittata has puffed up and is golden brown, 25 to 35 minutes.

5. Slice the frittata into 8 wedges. Serve immediately.

Shirred Eggs with Ham and Tomato

SHIRRED EGGS WITH HAM AND TOMATO

serves 1; recipe may be multiplied

This recipe, suitable for breakfast or a light lunch, is from chef David Waltuck of Chanterelle. Waltuck is best known for the innovative and elegant cuisine served at his groundbreaking restaurant, formerly in downtown New York City. Not as well known is the brief period when Chanterelle experimented with breakfast service. Simple yet luxurious, the dish epitomizes the Chanterelle approach. It makes one serving, so multiply amounts for additional servings desired. You'll need a mini 5-inch cast iron skillet for each serving.

1   tablespoon unsalted butter

2   slices Black Forest or other cooked ham, trimmed to fit pan

2   tablespoons tomato sauce, homemade or good-quality jarred

2   extra-large eggs

1   tablespoon heavy cream

Salt and freshly ground black pepper

1   teaspoon coarsely chopped fresh herbs (tarragon, chervil, and/or chives—just one herb or a mixture)

1. Preheat the oven to 350°.

2. Melt the butter in a 5-inch cast iron skillet over low heat. Remove the skillet from the heat.

3. Place the ham in the bottom of the pan. Spread the tomato sauce evenly over the ham. Carefully break the eggs on top; drizzle the cream over the eggs. Season with salt and pepper to taste (go very light on the salt since the ham is salty).

4. Place the pan in the oven and bake for 5 to 6 minutes, checking occasionally. The whites should be set, but the yolks can still be runny.

5. Sprinkle the eggs with the herbs and serve in the skillet.

Skillet Breakfast

SKILLET BREAKFAST

serves 4

Susan Stockton, Senior Vice President of Culinary Production for the Food Network and Cooking Channel, generally cooks for two to four people, so her 12-inch skillet gets a workout. She loves using it for baking cornbread and finishing a seared steak in the oven, but she also has found that its heat retention makes it the perfect oven-to-table vessel for this skillet breakfast. Feel free to use any kind of leftover cooked potato—russet, red, sweet, new, or whatever you have on hand.

1   tablespoon olive oil

1   small red onion, cut into   thin half-moons

1/2   red bell pepper, cut into thin strips

2   cooked potatoes, coarsely chopped

1   garlic clove, minced

1   (10-ounce) package frozen spinach, thawed and squeezed dry

1   teaspoon white wine vinegar

Salt and freshly ground black pepper

4   large eggs

1/2   cup grated Monterey Jack cheese

1/4   cup grated Parmesan cheese

1   ripe tomato, chopped

1. Preheat the oven to 375°.

2. Heat a 12-inch cast iron skillet over medium-high heat for a few minutes. Add the oil, onion, pepper strips, and chopped potatoes; cook, stirring occasionally, until the onion is softened and the potatoes crisp slightly. Add the garlic and cook a few minutes more.

3. After you've squeeze-dried the spinach, sprinkle it with white wine vinegar and make 4 "nests" to hold the eggs. Place them into the potato mixture. Season with salt and pepper.

4. Crack 1 egg into each nest and place the skillet in the oven; bake until the eggs are set, about 10 minutes.

5. Sprinkle the cheeses over the top and bake a few minutes more, until the cheeses melt.

6. Add salt to taste to the chopped tomato and sprinkle the tomato over the eggs. Wrap the handle of the pan with a doubled-up kitchen towel, bring it to the table, and serve.

crazy for cast iron

A 30-year-old 12-inch cast iron skillet lives on my cooktop, ready to go. It's old enough to have developed a great nonstick patina. My husband brought it to our first home along with an Acme juicer and a few copper pots. I was doubly impressed by the fact that not only did Rick cook, but he also clearly knew the value of quality cookware. — Susan Stockton

CHARLIE'S SCRAMBLED EGGS

serves 4

All of Charlie Pickens's family loves to cook in cast iron. His dad drives to the Lodge Factory Store in South Pittsburg, Tennessee, from Birmingham, Alabama, several times a year to buy skillet sets to give as gifts to family and friends.

6   large eggs

1   (14$^3/_4$-ounce) can cream-style corn

$^1/_2$ pound bacon slices, cooked, drained, and crumbled

2   tablespoons butter or canola oil

$^1/_4$ cup chopped onion

3   tablespoons chopped green bell pepper

1. Place the eggs in a large bowl and beat well. Stir in the corn and crumbled bacon.

2. Melt the butter in a 10-inch cast iron skillet over medium heat. Add the egg mixture and cook, stirring constantly. Add the onion and bell pepper just before the eggs are completely set.

BOB'S SLOW EGGS

Continuing his father's tradition, Robert Finch "Bob" Kellermann, CEO of Lodge, cooks the family breakfast on Sundays. Bob advises that the size of the skillet depends on how many eggs you'll be cooking—one dozen eggs will fit in a 10-inch skillet. He adds that it's important to cook the eggs over low heat, which means it will take time (typically 40 minutes to cook 18 eggs). If you're cooking a dozen or more eggs, you'll want to get them started before you fry the bacon or preheat the oven for biscuits, otherwise you'll be waiting on the eggs to finish when everything else is ready.

Bacon drippings or butter (2 to 3 tablespoons for a 10-inch skillet)

Eggs

Salt and freshly ground black pepper

Worcestershire sauce (2 dashes per egg)

Tabasco sauce (1 dash per egg)

Shredded sharp Cheddar cheese (about 1 cup per dozen eggs)

Paprika

1. Heat the bacon drippings in large cast iron skillet over low heat. Crack the eggs in the skillet, taking care not to break the yolks. Season to taste with salt and pepper, add the Worcestershire and Tabasco to each of the eggs, and sprinkle the cheese evenly over the top.

2. When the whites begin to cook, rake the bottom of the skillet with the edge of a fork, being careful not to break the yolks. Continue this process until the yolks start to cook; this folds the cheese into the softly cooked egg whites.

3. As the egg yolks begin to solidify, stir them into the other ingredients so you'll end up with yolk chunks that you wouldn't otherwise have.

4. Remove the skillet from the heat while the eggs are still too soft to serve; the heat from the skillet will continue to cook them. When the eggs have finished cooking (Bob likes them on the soft side), sprinkle them generously with paprika and serve them straight from the skillet.

Sunday Morning Ricotta Pancakes

SUNDAY MORNING RICOTTA PANCAKES

makes about 12 pancakes

When her kids were growing up, weekend breakfast meant eating together for Jan Hazard, who is a cookbook author and one half of the Kitchen GadgetGals. No gulping down orange juice and grabbing a toasted bagel—Jan's family looked forward to leisurely breakfasts and gabfests. This is one of her family's favorites: ricotta pancakes flavored with citrus zest. Serve them up with real maple or berry syrup.

2   cups all-purpose flour

2   tablespoons sugar

2   teaspoons baking powder

$^1/_2$ teaspoon baking soda

$^1/_2$ teaspoon salt

2   large eggs, separated

$1^1/_2$ cups milk

$^1/_2$ cup ricotta cheese

Grated zest of 1 orange or lemon

Light cooking oil

Maple or berry syrup

1. Combine the first 5 ingredients in a large bowl.

2. Beat the egg whites in a medium bowl with an electric mixer until soft peaks form; set aside. Combine the egg yolks, milk, and ricotta in another medium bowl and stir until smooth. Add the ricotta mixture to the flour mixture, stirring gently to combine. Fold in the beaten egg whites and zest with a rubber spatula just until there are no streaks of white left—the batter will be lumpy.

3. Heat a $10^1/_2$-inch cast iron griddle over medium heat until hot. Grease with a light cooking oil. Pour a scant $^1/_2$ cup of batter for each pancake onto the griddle and cook until bubbles form on the surface, about 2 minutes; turn and cook on the other side for 1 to 2 minutes, until lightly browned.

4. Serve immediately with maple or berry syrup or keep warm in a low-heat oven. Repeat with the remaining batter.

BUCKWHEAT PANCAKES

makes about 12 (4-inch) pancakes; serves 4

This recipe is from four-time James Beard-award-winning cookbook authors Bill Jamison and Cheryl Alters Jamison.

"Night Before" ingredients:

$1^1/_4$ cups milk, warm but not hot

1   teaspoon active dry yeast (about half envelope)

1   cup buckwheat flour

$^1/_2$ cup unbleached all-purpose flour

2   tablespoons stone-ground cornmeal

2   teaspoons brown sugar

$^1/_2$ teaspoon salt

"Morning" ingredients:

1   large egg, separated

$^1/_2$ teaspoon baking soda

About $^1/_4$ cup water

1   tablespoon unsalted butter, melted

Vegetable oil

Unsalted butter, softened

Real maple syrup or sorghum syrup, warmed

1. Begin making the batter the night before you plan to serve the pancakes. Pour the warm milk into a medium bowl, preferably one with a spout for pouring. Stir in the yeast and set the bowl aside briefly until the mixture begins to bubble. Stir in both flours, the cornmeal, brown sugar, and salt. Cover the bowl with a clean dish towel and refrigerate overnight.

2. The next morning, let the batter sit at room temperature for 15 to 30 minutes. Beat the egg white in a small bowl with an electric mixer until soft peaks form; set aside.

3. Add the egg yolk and baking soda to the batter and stir well; stir in enough water to make the batter pourable. Add the melted butter and stir until the butter disappears. Fold the beaten egg white into the batter until no white streaks remain.

4. Heat a cast iron griddle or large skillet over medium heat. Pour a thin film of oil on the griddle or into the skillet. Pour or spoon the batter onto the hot surface, where it should sizzle and hiss; 2 to 3 tablespoons of batter will make a 3-to 4-inch pancake. Make as many pancakes as you can fit on the surface without crowding.

5. Flip the pancakes just once after 1 to 2 minutes when the top surface is covered with bubbles but before all of the bubbles pop. (The bubbles will be fewer and larger for buckwheat pancakes than for wheat flour pancakes; the surface will look like Swiss cheese.) The pancakes are done when the second side is golden brown, another 1 to 2 minutes. Repeat with the remaining batter, adding a bit more oil to the griddle or skillet as needed. Serve immediately with butter and syrup.

{ buckwheat }

Probably brought to the American colonies by Dutch settlers, buckwheat pancakes became the most popular of all breakfast cakes in 19th-century America. They almost vanished in today's hyper-speed rush toward meals, but a renewed interest in grains has made them better known again. If buckwheat flour is not available at your grocery store, look for it at large supermarkets and natural food stores; coarser, grittier, and grayer than wheat flour, it is often sold in bulk. Buckwheat pancakes aren't complicated to make, but a good version demands overnight fermentation of the batter. The little extra time needed the evening before breakfast rewards you with a nutty, tangy, and toothsome pancake that is best prepared on a cast iron griddle or in a large shallow cast iron skillet.

Hannah's Apple Pancake

HANNAH'S APPLE PANCAKE

serves 1 generously

If you want your pancake to be really full of fruit, use two apples (the sautéing will be a little awkward at first, but the slices eventually cook down), and adjust the amount of sugar and cinnamon to taste. Cookbook editor Pam Hoenig adapted the original recipe in *The Breakfast Book* by Marion Cunningham to make just a single serving for her daughter, Hannah.

$^1/_4$ cup ($^1/_2$ stick) unsalted butter

$^1/_4$ cup milk

1 apple (Hannah prefers Golden Delicious)

2 tablespoons sugar

$^1/_2$ teaspoon ground cinnamon

1 large egg

$^1/_4$ cup all-purpose flour

Pinch of salt

1. Preheat the oven to 425°. Melt the butter in a 5-inch cast iron skillet over low heat.

2. While the butter melts, pour the milk into a 2-cup measuring cup. Peel the apple, then cut it off the core into 4 pieces. Cut each piece lengthwise into thin slices. In a small bowl, toss the apple slices with the sugar and cinnamon until well coated.

3. Pour half the melted butter into the milk and whisk well.

4. Add the apple slices and any loose sugar in the bowl to the hot butter in the skillet. Cook the apple slices over medium-low to low heat, turning them a few times, until softened; the sugar and butter will get nicely browned and bubbly. Remove the skillet from the heat.

5. Add the egg to the milk mixture and whisk to combine. Add the flour and salt and whisk until the batter is smooth. Pour the batter over the apples in the skillet, covering them.

6. Bake until the pancake puffs up and gets golden on top, with patches of brown, about 10 minutes. Enjoy the pancake straight from the skillet or invert it onto a serving plate.

a cast iron memory

When my mother-in-law, Constance Kingsley, passed away at the age of 88 and her household effects were being divided up, I made a beeline for her cast iron, which included 9-and $6^1/_2$-inch skillets. I have fond memories of my father-in-law, George Kingsley, cooking bacon in the larger skillet when we came to visit, but I had never seen him use the smaller one. I soon discovered my own use for it—baking a single-serving German pancake, my daughter Hannah's favorite breakfast food. Her Mimi and Poppy would be delighted with its new use.   —Pam Hoenig

Aebleskiver

AEBLESKIVER

makes 30 aebleskiver

Sarah Kirkwood "Pat" Lodge married the Rev. John Richard Lodge five years after they met at Auburn University during World War II. She enjoyed good food and exchanged recipes with many cooks in the parishes John served. Serve aebleskiver with maple syrup, jam, jelly or sprinkled with powdered sugar.

4   large eggs, separated

2   cups cake flour

1   tablespoon sugar

1   teaspoon baking powder

$1/2$ teaspoon salt

$1/4$ cup vegetable shortening, melted

Scant 2 cups milk (2 cups less 2 tablespoons)

1. In a large bowl, beat the egg yolks with an electric mixer until thick and pale. Wash and dry the beaters. In a medium bowl, beat the egg whites with the mixer until stiff peaks form.

2. In another medium bowl, sift together the flour, sugar, baking powder, and salt. Add dry ingredients alternately with melted shortening and milk to the beaten egg yolks. Lightly mix in the beaten egg whites with a whisk.

3. Heat a Lodge Aebleskiver Pan over medium heat. Brush a small amount of shortening or oil in each well and fill almost full with batter. Cook over medium heat until bubbly; using knitting needles, wooden skewers, or a small fondue fork, turn each one over after 30 seconds and continue to turn them every 30 seconds until all the sides are cooked to form a ball. Continue to turn them until browned on all sides. Remove from the pan.

4. Repeat with the remaining batter, then serve as you like.

FRENCH TOAST AND FRIED GREEN TOMATOES

serves 4

Born on the Joseph Lodge Farm, Barbara Gonce Clepper developed a passion early in life for cooking in cast iron and collecting both recipes and cast iron cookware. This recipe comes in handy for an overabundance of garden-fresh tomatoes. "We plant more than 30 tomato plants every summer," explains Barbara, "and this helps use up some of the tomatoes."

4   large eggs

$^1/_4$ cup milk

$^1/_4$ teaspoon salt

$^1/_8$ teaspoon freshly ground black pepper

4   bread slices

$^1/_4$ cup ($^1/_2$ stick) butter

3   medium green tomatoes, sliced

1. Place the eggs, milk, salt, and pepper in a large baking dish and beat well. Add the bread and let it soak until the egg mixture is absorbed, about 5 minutes on each side.

2. Heat a greased 12-inch cast iron griddle over medium-low heat. Add the bread slices and cook until browned on both sides.

3. While the bread slices are cooking, melt the butter in a 10-inch cast iron skillet over medium heat. Add the tomato slices and fry 3 minutes on each side.

4. For each serving, serve slices of fried tomato over each piece of French toast.

BERTHA'S CARROT-ZUCCHINI MUFFINS

makes 24 muffins

At 95 years old, Bertha Russell Gonce is still growing and picking her own zucchini. This recipe is a good way to use zucchini when it's quickly multiplying in your garden. These muffins are very good topped with cream cheese frosting.

1   cup all-purpose flour
1   cup whole wheat flour
$^3/_4$ cup firmly packed light brown sugar
1   teaspoon baking powder
1   teaspoon ground cinnamon
$^1/_2$ teaspoon salt
$^1/_2$ teaspoon baking soda
$^1/_4$ teaspoon ground allspice
1   large egg, beaten
$^3/_4$ cup orange juice
$^1/_2$ cup (1 stick) butter, melted
2   medium carrots, finely shredded
1   medium zucchini, finely shredded

1. Preheat the oven to 400°. Grease 2 (6-cup) cast iron muffin pans.

2. Combine both flours and the next 6 ingredients in a large bowl.

3. In a small bowl, stir together the egg, orange juice, and melted butter. Add to the dry ingredients, stirring just until moistened. Fold in the carrots and zucchini.

4. Spoon the batter into the prepared muffin pans, filling each well three-fourths full. Bake for 22 minutes. Remove the muffins from the pan immediately and cool completely on a wire rack.

5. Repeat with the remaining batter.

Ham and Sausage Muffins

HAM AND SAUSAGE MUFFINS

makes 12 muffins

These muffins from Martha Holland, who writes a weekly cooking column for her local paper, freeze very nicely. Let them cool completely, then freeze them in zip-top plastic freezer bags. To reheat, let the muffins thaw for about 15 minutes, wrap them tightly in aluminum foil, and place them in a preheated 400° oven for 15 minutes.

1 tablespoon butter

$^1/_4$ cup finely chopped green bell pepper

$^1/_4$ cup finely chopped green onions

$^1/_2$ cup plus 2 tablespoons all-purpose flour

$^1/_2$ cup yellow cornmeal

$^1/_2$ teaspoon baking soda

$^1/_2$ teaspoon salt

1 large egg

$^3/_4$ cup buttermilk

$^1/_3$ cup finely chopped ham

$^1/_3$ cup finely chopped cooked sausage

1. Preheat the oven to 400°. Grease 2 (6-cup) cast iron muffin pans.

2. In a small cast iron skillet, melt the butter and cook the bell pepper and green onions over medium heat until softened but not browned, stirring constantly.

3. In a large bowl, sift together the flour, cornmeal, baking soda, and salt. In a medium bowl, beat the egg, then stir in the buttermilk. Add the egg mixture to the flour mixture all at once, stirring only until blended; do not overstir. Carefully fold in the ham, sausage, and bell pepper mixture, along with any butter left in the skillet.

4. Spoon the batter into the prepared muffin pans, filling each well full. Bake until nicely browned, about 20 minutes. Cool in pans 5 minutes. Remove the muffins from the pans and cool completely on a wire rack.

Fresh Peach Crumb Coffee Cake

FRESH PEACH CRUMB COFFEE CAKE

serves 8

The cake is velvety, tender, and buttery, and the crumbs are big, dense, and sweet. It's an over-the-top rendition in the style David Bowers prefers in his cookbook *Bake It Like a Man: A Real Man's Cookbook*. With a layer of ripe peach slices (or plum, if you prefer) between the two layers, this is a real bakery-style coffee cake—the kind that makes you glad to face the morning. Served slightly warm with a scoop of vanilla ice cream, it also makes a fine dessert. For best results, remove any leftover cake from the skillet before storing.

Topping:

1½ cups all-purpose flour

½   cup firmly packed light brown sugar

½   cup granulated sugar

1½ teaspoons ground cinnamon

½   cup (1 stick) salted butter, melted

Cake:

½   cup (1 stick) salted butter, softened

½   cup granulated sugar

½   cup sour cream

2   large eggs

1½ teaspoons vanilla extract

1¼ cups all-purpose flour

½   teaspoon baking soda

½   teaspoon baking powder

1   pound ripe peaches (3 to 4 medium), peeled, pitted, and sliced

1. Preheat the oven to 350°. Liberally butter the bottom of a 10-inch cast iron skillet.

2. Place all the topping ingredients in a medium bowl and mix well to make a dense, smooth dough; set aside.

3. To make the cake batter, cream the butter and granulated sugar in a large bowl with an electric mixer until smooth. Add the sour cream, eggs, and vanilla and beat well. Place the flour, baking soda, and baking powder in a small bowl, stirring to combine; add to the batter all at once, stirring well to combine. The batter will be stiff.

4. Smooth the batter into the prepared skillet. Arrange the peach slices on top in a single layer. Crumble the topping mixture into big chunks and sprinkle on top of the peaches.

5. Bake until a toothpick inserted in the center comes out with crumbs clinging to it, about 45 minutes. (The cake will remain quite moist because of the peaches, but be sure you don't have streaks of raw batter on the toothpick.) Cool a little before cutting into wedges.

TOMATO GRITS

serves 6 to 8

In the South, grits are king. Cindy Schoeneck, who hails from Albertville, Alabama, says, "I recommend that 'newbies' try some type of cheese grits when you are first developing a taste for grits." This recipe is a variation of her cheese grits. "You can always omit the tomatoes if you want to try plain cheese grits. I also have added browned and crumbled sausage or bacon to make this more of a breakfast casserole."

2   cups water

$\frac{1}{4}$ cup milk

1   teaspoon salt

$\frac{1}{2}$ teaspoon freshly ground black pepper

1   cup quick-cooking grits

$\frac{1}{2}$ cup (1 stick) plus 1 tablespoon butter

1   medium onion, chopped

3   garlic cloves, minced

1   (10-ounce) can diced tomatoes and green chiles (such as Ro-tel), undrained

1   pound breakfast sausage or bacon, cooked, crumbled, and drained on paper towels (optional)

1   cup (4 ounces) shredded cheese (Cindy prefers an aged Cheddar or fontina)

1. Preheat the oven to 350°.

2. Combine the water and milk in a large saucepan; bring to a boil. Add the salt and pepper; slowly add the grits, whisking vigorously until the mixture returns to a boil. Add $\frac{1}{2}$ cup of the butter and continue to whisk constantly for 1 minute. Reduce the heat to low and simmer until the grits are thick and creamy, 3 to 5 minutes. Remove from the heat.

3. Melt the remaining 1 tablespoon butter in a deep $10\frac{1}{2}$-inch cast iron skillet or Dutch oven over medium heat. Add the onion and garlic and cook, stirring occasionally, until softened. Add the onion mixture, tomatoes, sausage, if desired, and $\frac{3}{4}$ cup of the cheese to the grits; stir well. Pour the mixture back into the skillet or Dutch oven and sprinkle with the remaining $\frac{1}{4}$ cup cheese. Place the skillet in the oven and bake until the grits are hot and bubbly and the cheese on top has melted, about 30 minutes.

crazy for cast iron

Cast iron cookware is a treasured possession in my family. Many pieces were passed down from one generation to the next and became "family heirlooms." I'm not sure how long this tradition has been going on—at least five generations. I know that my mother, Almyra McDill Engelman, and my aunt, Wendell McDill Thomason, were given cast iron skillets from my great-grandmother when they were married. Today, I have one of my mother's wedding gift cast iron skillets. I enjoy collecting "aged" and antique cast iron cookware, too. I own several skillets, a Dutch oven, a griddle, and three cornstick pans. I have a cast iron skillet designated for "bread and vegetables" and one for "meats" because breads and vegetables tend to stick in skillets where meats have been cooked. I have found that nonstick cooking sprays do not add to the seasoning of the pan, so I use unsalted butter to grease my cookware and vegetable oil to season them. If you find that your prized cast iron piece has started to rust, just scrub off the rust with a dish scrubber and warm dish detergent, then reseason the pan with a generous coating of vegetable oil. — Cindy Schoeneck

GRANNY'S SAUSAGE AND GRAVY

serves 6

This gravy is sometimes called country gravy or milk gravy. In the early 1900s, it was the usual breakfast food served at logging camps, where they started calling it sawmill gravy. Today it's popular poured over big, hot biscuits and served for breakfast, lunch, or dinner. This version is from Vickie Davenport. If you make the gravy in a Lodge Combo Cooker, use the lid to bake your biscuits.

1   pound bulk pork breakfast sausage

1   tablespoon canola oil

3   tablespoons all-purpose flour

$1^{1}/_{2}$ cups milk (or more as needed)

Salt and freshly ground black pepper

1. Cook the sausage in a large, deep cast iron skillet or in the bottom of a Lodge Combo Cooker over medium-high heat, stirring until it crumbles and is no longer pink. Remove the sausage and drain on paper towels, leaving 1 to $1^{1}/_{2}$ tablespoons of drippings in the skillet. Add oil to pan.

2. Sprinkle the flour over the drippings and oil in the pan and cook over medium heat, stirring constantly, until the flour is browned. Add the milk, $^{1}/_{2}$ cup at a time, and cook until the gravy has the consistency you prefer. Stir in the sausage, season with salt and pepper to taste, and serve.

TOMATO GRAVY

serves 4

There are many different recipes for tomato gravy, or "mater

gravy" as it is often called. It is good over biscuits for breakfast, lunch, or dinner. The secret is to constantly stir it—if you leave it for a second, it will lump up.

Drippings from 2 cooked bacon slices

2   large ripe tomatoes, finely chopped

1   large Vidalia onion, chopped

Dash of Tabasco sauce

$1/_2$ teaspoon salt

$1/_4$ teaspoon freshly ground black pepper

$1/_4$ cup all-purpose flour

1   cup leftover coffee

1. Heat bacon drippings in a well-seasoned 12-inch cast iron skillet over medium-high heat. Add the tomatoes and onion, stirring until the onion is softened, about 5 minutes. Add the Tabasco, salt, and pepper. Add the flour and cook, stirring constantly, until the mixture thickens.

2. Gradually add the coffee and bring the mixture to a boil, stirring constantly. Reduce the heat to medium-low and cook until thickened, about 5 minutes, stirring constantly. Serve as desired.

SOUP, STEW, GUMBO & CHILI

Nothing says comfort like a pot of soup or chili simmering away on the back burner of your stove. This chapter offers a wonderful collection of regional specialties that extend the length and breadth of the United States.

Southern Greens Soup

SOUTHERN GREENS SOUP

serves 4

This recipe is from Louise S. "Lou" Fuller, wife of Ed Fuller, president of the National Cornbread Festival, which is held each year in Lodge's hometown, South Pittsburg, Tennessee. Of course, Lou likes to serve this soup with hot cornbread!

2   tablespoons canola oil

1   medium onion, chopped

4   cups water

1   envelope dry vegetable soup mix (such as Knorr's)

2   pounds fresh turnip greens, washed, drained, and chopped

1   (20-ounce) can white beans, drained

1   (14-to 16-ounce) package Polish sausage, sliced

Hot water (optional)

1. Heat the oil in a 7-quart cast iron Dutch oven over medium-high heat; add the onion and cook until softened, stirring occasionally. Add the water and soup mix, stirring to combine. Bring to a boil and simmer 5 minutes.

2. Add the turnip greens and simmer 10 minutes.

3. Add the beans and sausage; simmer until the greens are tender, about 15 minutes. If you want the soup more "soupy," add hot water a little at a time until desired consistency.

TEX-MEX MINESTRONE

serves 6 to 8

This quick and hearty one-dish meal was contributed by International Dutch Oven Society member Debbie Hair.

1   pound lean ground beef

3   cups water

1   (28-ounce) can crushed tomatoes

1   (15-ounce) can black beans, drained and rinsed

1½ cups frozen or canned corn, thawed and drained 1   (14½-ounce) can beef broth ½   cup zesty Italian dressing 1   teaspoon ground cumin

1   cup small pasta shells

1   cup shredded Colby-Jack cheese

1. Brown the beef in a 12-inch cast iron Dutch oven over high heat, stirring often, until the meat crumbles and is no longer pink; drain.

2. Add the water and the next 6 ingredients; stir to combine. Bring to a boil; add the pasta, reduce the heat to medium, and simmer until pasta is just tender, about 8 minutes.

3. Sprinkle cheese over the top of each serving.